Spiritual
Boot
Camp

Jeremiah J. Guendoo

Orders

In December 2023, I received direct orders from our commander-in-chief, King Jesus. These orders were a call to deeper consecration with God, which would lead His people into the next level of spiritual warriors.

December 14th, 2023

There is something unsettling in the spiritual atmosphere. There is an event taking place that will lay a foundation for life to change as we know it. The Lord spoke to me about His Church through the book of Joel. Allow me to lay out the context first. In Joel 1:9-20, it reads:

> *9 The meat offering and the drink offering is cut off from the house of the LORD; the priests, the LORD's ministers, mourn. 10 The field is wasted, the land mourneth; for the corn is wasted: the new wine is dried up, the oil languisheth. 11 Be ye ashamed, O ye husbandmen; howl, O ye vinedressers, for the wheat and for the barley; because the harvest of the field is perished. 12 The vine is dried up, and the fig tree languisheth; the pomegranate tree, the palm tree also, and the apple tree, even all the trees of the field, are withered: because joy is withered away from the sons of men. 13 Gird yourselves, and lament, ye priests: howl, ye ministers of the altar: come, lie all night in sackcloth, ye ministers of my God: for the meat offering and the drink offering is withholden from the house of your God. 14 Sanctify ye a fast, call a solemn assembly, gather the elders and all the inhabitants of the land into the house of the LORD your God, and cry unto the LORD, 15 Alas for the day! for the day of the LORD is at hand, and as a destruction from the Almighty shall it come. 16 Is not the meat cut off before our eyes, yea, joy and gladness from the house of our God? 17 The seed is rotten under their clods, the garners are laid desolate, the barns are broken down; for the corn is*

withered.¹⁸ How do the beasts groan! the herds of cattle are perplexed, because they have no pasture; yea, the flocks of sheep are made desolate.¹⁹ O LORD, to thee will I cry: for the fire hath devoured the pastures of the wilderness, and the flame hath burned all the trees of the field.²⁰ The beasts of the field cry also unto thee: for the rivers of waters are dried up, and the fire hath devoured the pastures of the wilderness.

(Joel 1:9-20, KJV)

We learn of the widespread destruction and desolation across the land. Following this devastation, the people were called to a profound place of consecration, prayer, and fasting. Subsequently, in Joel 2:1-11, we read,

2 Blow ye the trumpet in Zion, and sound an alarm in my holy mountain: let all the inhabitants of the land tremble: for the day of the LORD cometh, for it is nigh at hand;² A day of darkness and of gloominess, a day of clouds and of thick darkness, as the morning spread upon the mountains: a great people and a strong; there hath not been ever the like, neither shall be any more after it, even to the years of many generations.³ A fire devoureth before them; and behind them a flame burneth: the land is as the garden of Eden before them, and behind them a desolate wilderness; yea, and nothing shall escape them.⁴ The appearance of them is as the appearance of horses; and as horsemen, so shall they run.⁵ Like the noise of chariots on the tops of mountains shall they leap, like the noise of a flame of fire that devoureth the stubble, as a strong people set in battle array.⁶ Before their face the people shall be much pained: all faces shall gather blackness.⁷ They shall run like mighty men; they shall climb the wall like men of war; and they shall march every one on his ways, and they shall not break their ranks:⁸ Neither shall one thrust another; they shall walk every one in his path: and when they fall upon the sword, they shall not be wounded.⁹ They shall run to and fro in the city; they shall run upon the wall, they shall climb up upon the houses; they shall enter in at the windows like a thief.¹⁰ The earth shall quake before them; the heavens shall tremble: the sun and the moon shall be dark, and the stars shall withdraw their shining:¹¹ And the LORD shall utter his voice before his army: for his camp is very great: for he is strong that executeth his word: for the day of the LORD is great and very terrible; and who can abide it?

(Joel 2:1-11, KJV)

This is an unstoppable and fearsome army sent by God. Once the army was released, there was restoration from the destruction (Joel 2:25), and the Spirit would be poured out (Joel 2:28-30).

²⁵ And I will restore to you the years that the locust hath eaten, the cankerworm, and the caterpiller, and the palmerworm, my great army which I sent among you. ²⁸ And it shall come to pass afterward, that I will pour out my spirit upon all flesh; and your sons and your daughters shall prophesy, your old men shall dream dreams, your young men shall see visions:²⁹ And also upon the servants and upon the handmaids in those days will I pour out my spirit.³⁰ And I will shew wonders in the heavens and in the earth, blood, and fire, and pillars of smoke.

(Joel 2:25,28-30, KJV)

Here is what the Lord said to me: This word is not a fulfillment of the prophecies in Joel but rather a typological outline of what we will experience in the years to come. Just as there was destruction in Joel 1:9-20, there will be destruction, desolation, and hardship in the land. Struggles will be evident in both the secular world and the church world. This turmoil simultaneously serves as a call to the Church for deeper consecration, prayer, and fasting, just as we read in Joel 1:13-14. From this radical consecration, a battle-hardened army will be produced and released by God. This refers to us, the equipped church, as indicated in Mark 16:17-18, Matthew 10:1, 7-8, Acts 1:8, and 1 John 3:8. The release of this army will lead to the restoration of things lost (Joel 2:25), harvest, outpouring of the Holy Ghost, and miracles (Joel 2:28-30). However, it all begins with the people of God turning to prayer and fasting in a time of desolation. This transformation will forge us into battle-hardened individuals. Only then will we witness what God has promised us. In preparation for the impending hardship and to begin the process of becoming a spiritual, battle-hardened army, the Lord is calling His people to this Spiritual Boot Camp.

Jeremiah J. Guendoo

Spiritual Evolutions

In the military, they refer to a training exercise or maneuver as an "evolution." In our spiritual boot camp, there will be evolutions that we develop. Sometimes, these evolutions are more than just exercises; they are maneuvers performed that have practical use in combat. If an exercise is performed only once, it provides little to no lasting benefit. Lasting benefits are found when the exercise is done often and consistently.

Possibly the most important thing that the church needs to develop is consistency. Many struggles with consistency, even outside of things of spiritual benefit. In Ezekiel, God spoke to the writer

As an adamant harder than flint have I made thy forehead:

(Ezekial 3:9, KJV)

This was an admonishment to the prophet, indicating that he was being given resilience to face adversity and challenges. This is the mindset you must adopt when entering this spiritual boot camp. There will be times when you will not want to pray, read your Bible, fast, or consecrate. There will be times when you will want to binge-watch YouTube videos instead of engaging in a time of prayer. However, you must possess a stubborn determination that, in the face of every call to compromise, you will accomplish the evolutions that have been laid out before you. Have a determination that you WILL NOT go to sleep until you have been faithful in your commitments to consecration.

.

Brothers-In-Arms

It is a true saying that some of the deepest bonds ever formed are with people who have gone through hardship and adversity with you. My father served in the U.S. Navy, working on the flight deck of aircraft carriers. This was an extremely dangerous environment. My father shared numerous stories with me about the times he almost got hit during landing and other dangers of the environment. When he and some of his old sailor friends get together, it could have been years since they last spoke, but the kindred spirit still resonates between them because of what they experienced together. At times, there are even people who worked on the ship (but not on the flight deck) who attend these reunions. Even though they all knew each other, there was exclusivity with the team that worked on the flight deck. A bond was forged in these hardships and adversity.

I implore you to find a brother or sister in arms with whom you can undertake this boot camp. Let it be someone who can challenge, encourage, and hold you accountable during this boot camp. There will be times when you are going to be too tired or exhausted to pray. But Ecclesiastes says,

For if they fall, the one will lift up his fellow:

(Ecclesiastes 4:10, KJV)

It is the encouragement of a brother or sister in Christ that will pick you up and challenge you to pray that keep you consistent when you feel you cannot continue.

Jeremiah J. Guendoo

Prayer

There are certain places in God we can only reach by times of deep of venturing into the deep places of God. In Job, it says,

or hast thou walked in the search of the depth?

(Job 38:16, KJV)

This is a spiritual challenge going forth to the church world today. To reach the deep places takes time. When some voyaged to reach the bottom of the Mariana Trench (the deepest place on Earth), it took over two and a half hours. The deep places in God are found in deep places of prayer, not just praying fifteen to twenty minutes a day but engaging in two, three, and even four hours of prayer. This does not necessarily mean we are going to pray for four hours straight (although this could happen). When I pray for three hours a day, it is often because I have broken it up into segments: two hours in the morning and 1 in the evening, even praying for one hour at every mealtime.

There are rare species of fish and precious materials found in the deepest parts of the ocean. The most precious metals and ores are found in deep places in caves. The Psalmist says,

23 They that go down to the sea in ships, that do business in great waters;24 These see the works of the LORD, and his wonders in the deep.

(Psalm 107:23-24, KJV)

In the deep places of prayer, wonders, powerful works of God, and anointing are found. There are material blessings,

14

answered prayers, and miracles that are discovered in these deep places of prayer.

As I have previously mentioned, many precious stones and ores are found in caves. In the Bible, we read about how David and his mighty men lived in the Cave of Adullam. The true army and people of God resided, lived, and made their abode in the cave. This is where the army of God must dwell—in the cave. When King Saul entered the cave, he was unable to see any of the men living there because he had not gone deep enough. Perhaps if he had gone farther, David and his men would have been revealed. I want to go deep into the cave of His presence! I want to be like Ezekiel and swim in the river, not just stay where it is at ankle level.

Why does a particular hour or hours matter in prayer? Doesn't this almost seem Pharisaical? Well, it is certainly easy for it to become that way. However, we must look at our own life and think about the struggle, temptation, and warfare that we go through on an everyday basis. Consider whether it is easy or difficult to hear the voice of God. If you are always under attack and can never hear from God, it could be because there has not been enough spiritual activity demonstrated on your behalf. If I begin to struggle, I look at my personal devotion. The more lackadaisical I am in my personal walk, often the more I begin to struggle.

However, it can seem discouraging to attempt to journey into deeper areas of prayer when we feel nothing is happening. Firstly, there are times when we need to subject our flesh and make it go further in prayer. Even when we do not feel it, we must press on. However, there are ways to make prayer more effective. Here are some pointers I learned from studying some of the work of Rev. Verbal Bean.

Firstly, I start all prayer by covering these four things that Daniel prayed:

O Lord, hear; O Lord, forgive; O Lord, hearken and do; defer not, for thine own sake, O my God: for thy city and thy people are called by thy name.

(Daniel 9:19,KJV)

Oh Lord, Hear – This is a time to focus your mind on God. You get God's attention by making sure he knows he has your attention. Put out distractions of the world and zone in on God.

Oh Lord, Forgive – This is a time of repentance and asking for forgiveness. Make sure the slate is clean and sin is dealt with. Undealt with sin can hinder times of prayer and communication with God.

Oh Lord, Hearken – Hearkening is different from hearing. Hearing is you putting your attention on God. Hearkening is now asking God to put his attention on you. That he would let his presence and abode rest in where you are at

Do, and Defer not – Ask that the prayers which you speak to God are not just heard, but quickly performed. That our heavenly Father would be swift to action on the things we request and petition.

This alone could easily be twenty to thirty minutes of prayer. I then begin to transition into a time of worship, just enjoying the presence of God. Do not get in a hurry to get to your prayer requests but enjoy spending time with your heavenly Father. Often, some of our prayers are answered when we just abide in His presence.

In the Old Testament, we see it demonstrated that a king had to be approached in a specific way. A servant, child, or even a spouse could not just rush in. This is a typology of how we approach God. It is like channels on a walkie-talkie. If I want to talk to my friend on channel two, I am not going to tune into channel eight. When we are in prayer, we must begin to search out the channels that God is wanting us to approach. When we find it, that is the area we focus on. There are four channels the Bible talks about.

Prayer (Communion) – (After my time of worship, I typically begin with communion. This is where we talk with God. Speaking to him about our everyday life, like a friend to a friend. There is not much emotion or warfare but speaking plainly. Even taking time to meditate and allow for him to speak back

Thanksgiving – A time of worship. In thanksgiving, not only do I thank God for what he has done, but for what he is going to do. I have found that thanksgiving is often the channel God wants to speak to me on when I am feeling doubtful or lacking in faith. Thanksgiving is the language of faith. This can often have more emotion involved and time of relief and excitement.

Supplication(Petition) – This is when we begin to petition God for the things we need in our life. Whether it be deliverance, breakthrough, a miracle, or finances. There can be more emotion involved where we begin to petition God and claim things back from the enemy.

Intercession- Intercession is standing in the gap for someone or their need. Intercession has heavy emotion, travail, and warfare that is involved. Often intercession is not things that we pray in the natural but pray in our heavenly language. This is the Spirit helping our infirmities.

How does one begin to find which channel to pray on? Sometimes, you will already feel in your spirit which channel God is on. Begin to pray and commune with God, then start to enter each channel individually. Transition into petition and feel after God. If you are not feeling anything or any breakthrough, transition to thanksgiving or intercession. When you begin to pray through and really tap into the presence of God, that is when you know you have found the correct channel. In prayer, I always attempt to press in and get breakthrough. But there are other times where God just wants communion and fellowship. It is not time for warfare, or pleading, but just speaking with Him. Some prayer sessions, you will go into all four channels. Other sessions, you may only enter one. This will help you be more effective in prayer and learn sensitivity to the leading of the Spirit.

Jeremiah J. Guendoo

Fasting

Fasting is one of the most effective things that a person can do. Fasting is the very thing that the flesh hates the most. I know of many who know the power of fasting, but this does not mean that their flesh enjoys it! Whenever we fast, we are beginning to show God just how serious we are about the things we need. There are things that fasting can get done with more speed than just simply prayer. (It is important to note that we must always couple prayer and fasting. Never attempt to fast if you have not been praying or will not pray). There are typically four main reasons to fast.

First, we should fast to have a deeper communion with God. Elijah fasted for forty days in preparation for the encounter he was going to have when he heard the still small voice. Moses fasted for forty days and saw a greater manifestation of the presence of God. Fasting will bring us closer to God.

Second, fasting will unlock power and authority. Jesus even stated that,

[21] Howbeit this kind goeth not out but by prayer and fasting.

(Matthew 17:21, KJV)

Fasting is a way to gain authority in the Spirit and see the power of God flow through you. There is no shortcut or way around it. Before Jesus was ever used in a single miracle, he went on a forty day fast.

Thirdly, Fasting is a way to subject the flesh and get authority over struggles and temptations. In Ezra, it says,

Then I proclaimed a fast there, at the river of Ahava, that we might afflict ourselves before our God

(Ezra 8:21, KJV)

If you are struggling with fleshly temptation and battle, or just feel you have become more carnal, fasting is a way to subdue the flesh. It is as if you are telling your flesh, "You have gotten out of control; now, I am going to exercise my power over you by making you not eat."

Lastly, in the book of Esther, we read about how she fasted on behalf of a situation where her people were facing extermination. She was so serious that she went on a fast for three days where she drank no water and ate no food. This queen understood that when nothing else would work, fasting would. It was to see God move on behalf of her situation. If there is a dire situation where someone needs a miracle or intervention, it is time to proclaim a fast.

Fasting always includes not eating. There are forms of consecration where one will not eat sugar, drink sweet drinks, or eat junk food. This is consecration that God honors, but it is not a fast. Here are diverse ways one can fast. Fasting is typically done by only drinking water. However, if you are someone who works a highly active lifestyle, I would recommend drinking something to replenish electrolytes (such as Propel), and once or twice a day drinking a bowl of vegetable broth. Before you ever go on a fast, be sure to know your reason for doing the fast.

There are times when I fast that I have a comprehensive list of things I fast toward. Fast with a purpose.

Sun-up to Sun-down – This is simply not eating during the time that the sun is up. This is what they did in the bible whenever they proclaimed a fast, (Unless it was explicitly stated they fasted for _____ days and nights)

Absolute fast – This is when someone eats no food for an entire period they are awake. This is what is referenced when in the Bible it mentions they fasted for a certain amount of days and nights.

Extended fast – An absolute fast that goes beyond three days. Typical increments are 7 days, 10 days, 14 days, 21 days, and 40 days. When a person goes into time of extended fasting, it is because they are fasting for a definite purpose. If you are feeling led to do an extended fast, have a definite word from God and speak with your Pastor about it.

Jeremiah J. Guendoo

Bible Reading and Memorization

It is impossible for a plane to fly without a wing on each side. In the same way, our spirituality is a plane, and the wing on one side is prayer, while the wing on the other side is reading the Word of God. The Word of God is our only weapon that has been given to us to fight (since it is the sword of the Spirit). The Word of God keeps us in alignment from getting into activities that are counter to the nature of God.

It is of the utmost importance that we begin to saturate ourselves in the Bible. Many of us do bread charts where we read the Bible in an entire year. I am not against this at all. However, how often does it happen where we cannot recall the scripture we read three, two, or even one day prior? We must become more effective in our ability to digest and absorb the Word of God.

When we do our daily Bible reading or bread chart, on top of the reading, do a time of study to understand. There are numerous ways we can study our Bible to be more effective.

Original Language – Get understanding about the original languages of Hebrew and Greek that the Bible was written in. There are troves of gold nuggets found when we begin to research the original language. There are different translations, or even Strong's concordance that can help with this.

Historical Context – Since the Bible is not written in a synonymous timeline, it can be beneficial to read the Bible in an actual chronological order. Another thing one can do is to find the time when certain books were written and see if you can find a worldview of what was happening through the entirety of humanity during this time.

Cultural Understanding – Much of the Bible is lost in translation or misunderstood because we do not have the eastern culture's frame of view. When we study the actual culture of the time, this brings new revelation on why different language and actions are inserted into the text.

Geographical competency – Often when we read about places or locations in the Bible, we can often brush over it and not pay attention. But when we try to understand the geography of the text it can give us a better immersive experience into the Word of God. When we can see how stories overlap at the same location or understand the location of different nations and tribes will give us a better-rounded view of the scripture.

Another crucial tool is to memorize scriptures and chapters. When Jesus was fasting for 40 days, he did not have a Bible with Him. When Satan came tempting Jesus, it was the scripture that he had memorized that allowed him to dismantle the attack of the enemy. When we memorize a text, it becomes a part of us. When we rehearse it throughout our everyday life there can be new life and meaning that begins to take on the verse. It is much easier to live verses out when we have them committed to memory.

Jeremiah J. Guendoo

Consecration and Media Fast

When a soldier enters boot camp, it is a time of focusing on the task at hand. Recruits are unable to eat food from the outside world, have extremely limited access to television only during their free time, and limited access to the outside world. There are no personal devices or access to social media permitted during boot camp.

During our time of spiritual boot camp, it is time to tighten up on our everyday walk and life. This is the time to attain victory over various habits and addictions against which we have battled. You can even take this time to create new healthy habits such as clean eating and exercise. One could begin to make a habit of reading a book every day. Use it as a time to holistically recreate and shape your life. Take an account of your life every day and how you spend your time.

It should be a sincere desire within our heart to be righteous and holy before God. Every day, look at your life and actions. Pray that God begins to convict you of things that grieve the Spirit. Pray that He will take you deeper into habits that will glorify Him in everyday life.

If soldiers in boot camp do not get on social media and have limited access to entertainment, why should it be any different for us entering a spiritual boot camp? Some of the tasks that we are going to attempt to complete may seem unfeasible because of our lack of time. However, one would be surprised how much time they have when we begin to cut out indulgence in social media and entertainment.

Jeremiah J. Guendoo

Prerequisite Phase

Before a recruit enters boot camp, there is a list of prerequisites he must accomplish before entry is permitted: fifty push-ups, fifty sit-ups, ten pull-ups, etc. We do not want to give ourselves unrealistic expectations if we do not already have a consistent relationship with God. This initial phase is to have a time of consistency that will prepare us for boot camp. The prerequisite phase is thirty days of spiritual consistency. Here are the assignments.

Pray one-two hours a day

Can be accomplished by praying 30 minutes in the morning and 30 minutes in the evening. Progression in prayer comes naturally once the habit is developed.

Daily Bible reading plus thirty minutes of study

Read the equivalent of a three-hundred and sixty-give bible reading plan (or whatever your daily reading is.) On top of this do 30 minutes of study and research of what you read. Change the framework of reading. Do not read to check the list off. Read to try to learn, engraft, and understand. Utilize google, concordance, and approved translations to have a well-rounded understanding of scripture.

Memorize one verse every two weeks

Try to learn one verse every two weeks. This will help the process of living out and becoming the Word (Romans 12:1-2)

Fast once a week

Attempt to go one day a week without eating any food. If you cannot do that, attempt to do a sunrise to sunset fast where you do not eat any food while the sun is up.

Limit social media and entertainment to one hour a day

Social media and entertainment have become one of the greatest hindrances to the people of God in the twenty-first century. It is easy to waste time on media and entertainment or fall prey to sin and carnality. One would be surprised as to how much time they spend on media. Limit your time on social media, and indulging entertainment to one hour a day.

Included for our everyday checklist is also a space where you can write about what God spoke to you in prayer, what stuck out to you during time of Bible reading, or even the victories and struggles of the day. (On the daily checklist there is no checkmark for fasting. It will be up to you to look over your schedule and choose what day to fast every week.)

DAY 1

- Pray 1-2 hours ☐
- Daily Bible reading ☐
- 30 minutes of Biblical study ☐
- Work on scripture memorization ☐
- One hour or less of media and entertainment ☐

_____
_____
_____
_____
_____
_____
_____
_____
_____
_____
_____
_____
_____
_____

DAY 2

- Pray 1-2 hours ☐
- Daily Bible reading ☐
- 30 minutes of Biblical study ☐
- Work on scripture memorization ☐
- One hour or less of media and entertainment ☐

_____
_____
_____
_____
_____
_____
_____
_____
_____
_____
_____
_____
_____

DAY 3

- Pray 1-2 hours ☐
- Daily Bible reading ☐
- 30 minutes of Biblical study ☐
- Work on scripture memorization ☐
- One hour or less of media and entertainment ☐

_____
_____
_____
_____
_____
_____
_____
_____
_____
_____
_____
_____
_____
_____

DAY 4

- Pray 1-2 hours ☐
- Daily Bible reading ☐
- 30 minutes of Biblical study ☐
- Work on scripture memorization ☐
- One hour or less of media and entertainment ☐

DAY 5

- Pray 1-2 hours ☐
- Daily Bible reading ☐
- 30 minutes of Biblical study ☐
- Work on scripture memorization ☐
- One hour or less of media and entertainment ☐

_____
_____
_____
_____
_____
_____
_____
_____
_____
_____
_____
_____
_____
_____

DAY 6

- Pray 1-2 hours ☐
- Daily Bible reading ☐
- 30 minutes of Biblical study ☐
- Work on scripture memorization ☐
- One hour or less of media and entertainment ☐

_____
_____
_____
_____
_____
_____
_____
_____
_____
_____
_____
_____
_____

DAY 7

- Pray 1-2 hours ☐
- Daily Bible reading ☐
- 30 minutes of Biblical study ☐
- Work on scripture memorization ☐
- One hour or less of media and entertainment ☐

_____
_____
_____
_____
_____
_____
_____
_____
_____
_____
_____
_____
_____
_____

DAY 8

- Pray 1-2 hours ☐
- Daily Bible reading ☐
- 30 minutes of Biblical study ☐
- Work on scripture memorization ☐
- One hour or less of media and entertainment ☐

_____
_____
_____
_____
_____
_____
_____
_____
_____
_____
_____
_____
_____

DAY 9

- Pray 1-2 hours ☐
- Daily Bible reading ☐
- 30 minutes of Biblical study ☐
- Work on scripture memorization ☐
- One hour or less of media and entertainment ☐

_____
_____
_____
_____
_____
_____
_____
_____
_____
_____
_____
_____
_____

DAY 10

- Pray 1-2 hours ☐
- Daily Bible reading ☐
- 30 minutes of Biblical study ☐
- Work on scripture memorization ☐
- One hour or less of media and entertainment ☐

_____
_____
_____
_____
_____
_____
_____
_____
_____
_____
_____
_____
_____

DAY 11

- Pray 1-2 hours ☐
- Daily Bible reading ☐
- 30 minutes of Biblical study ☐
- Work on scripture memorization ☐
- One hour or less of media and entertainment ☐

_____
_____
_____
_____
_____
_____
_____
_____
_____
_____
_____
_____
_____

DAY 12

- Pray 1-2 hours ☐
- Daily Bible reading ☐
- 30 minutes of Biblical study ☐
- Work on scripture memorization ☐
- One hour or less of media and entertainment ☐

_____
_____
_____
_____
_____
_____
_____
_____
_____
_____
_____
_____
_____
_____
_____

DAY 13

- Pray 1-2 hours ☐
- Daily Bible reading ☐
- 30 minutes of Biblical study ☐
- Work on scripture memorization ☐
- One hour or less of media and entertainment ☐

_____
_____
_____
_____
_____
_____
_____
_____
_____
_____
_____
_____
_____
_____

DAY 14

- Pray 1-2 hours ☐
- Daily Bible reading ☐
- 30 minutes of Biblical study ☐
- Work on scripture memorization ☐
- One hour or less of media and entertainment ☐

_____
_____
_____
_____
_____
_____
_____
_____
_____
_____
_____
_____
_____

DAY 15

- Pray 1-2 hours ☐
- Daily Bible reading ☐
- 30 minutes of Biblical study ☐
- Work on scripture memorization ☐
- One hour or less of media and entertainment ☐

_____
_____
_____
_____
_____
_____
_____
_____
_____
_____
_____
_____
_____
_____
_____

DAY 16

- Pray 1-2 hours ☐
- Daily Bible reading ☐
- 30 minutes of Biblical study ☐
- Work on scripture memorization ☐
- One hour or less of media and entertainment ☐

_____
_____
_____
_____
_____
_____
_____
_____
_____
_____
_____
_____
_____
_____
_____

DAY 17

- Pray 1-2 hours ☐
- Daily Bible reading ☐
- 30 minutes of Biblical study ☐
- Work on scripture memorization ☐
- One hour or less of media and entertainment ☐

_____
_____
_____
_____
_____
_____
_____
_____
_____
_____
_____
_____
_____
_____

DAY 18

- Pray 1-2 hours ☐
- Daily Bible reading ☐
- 30 minutes of Biblical study ☐
- Work on scripture memorization ☐
- One hour or less of media and entertainment ☐

_____
_____
_____
_____
_____
_____
_____
_____
_____
_____
_____
_____
_____

DAY 19

- Pray 1-2 hours ☐
- Daily Bible reading ☐
- 30 minutes of Biblical study ☐
- Work on scripture memorization ☐
- One hour or less of media and entertainment ☐

_____

_____

_____

_____

_____

_____

_____

_____

_____

_____

_____

_____

_____

DAY 20

- Pray 1-2 hours ☐
- Daily Bible reading ☐
- 30 minutes of Biblical study ☐
- Work on scripture memorization ☐
- One hour or less of media and entertainment ☐

_____
_____
_____
_____
_____
_____
_____
_____
_____
_____
_____
_____
_____
_____

DAY 21

- Pray 1-2 hours ☐
- Daily Bible reading ☐
- 30 minutes of Biblical study ☐
- Work on scripture memorization ☐
- One hour or less of media and entertainment ☐

_____

_____

_____

_____

_____

_____

_____

_____

_____

_____

_____

_____

_____

DAY 21

- Pray 1-2 hours ☐
- Daily Bible reading ☐
- 30 minutes of Biblical study ☐
- Work on scripture memorization ☐
- One hour or less of media and entertainment ☐

DAY 23

- Pray 1-2 hours ☐
- Daily Bible reading ☐
- 30 minutes of Biblical study ☐
- Work on scripture memorization ☐
- One hour or less of media and entertainment ☐

_____
_____
_____
_____
_____
_____
_____
_____
_____
_____
_____
_____
_____
_____

DAY 24

- Pray 1-2 hours ☐
- Daily Bible reading ☐
- 30 minutes of Biblical study ☐
- Work on scripture memorization ☐
- One hour or less of media and entertainment ☐

_____
_____
_____
_____
_____
_____
_____
_____
_____
_____
_____
_____
_____

DAY 25

- Pray 1-2 hours ☐
- Daily Bible reading ☐
- 30 minutes of Biblical study ☐
- Work on scripture memorization ☐
- One hour or less of media and entertainment ☐

_____
_____
_____
_____
_____
_____
_____
_____
_____
_____
_____
_____
_____
_____

DAY 26

- Pray 1-2 hours ☐
- Daily Bible reading ☐
- 30 minutes of Biblical study ☐
- Work on scripture memorization ☐
- One hour or less of media and entertainment ☐

_____
_____
_____
_____
_____
_____
_____
_____
_____
_____
_____
_____
_____
_____

DAY 27

- Pray 1-2 hours ☐
- Daily Bible reading ☐
- 30 minutes of Biblical study ☐
- Work on scripture memorization ☐
- One hour or less of media and entertainment ☐

_____
_____
_____
_____
_____
_____
_____
_____
_____
_____
_____
_____
_____

DAY 28

- Pray 1-2 hours ☐
- Daily Bible reading ☐
- 30 minutes of Biblical study ☐
- Work on scripture memorization ☐
- One hour or less of media and entertainment ☐

_____
_____
_____
_____
_____
_____
_____
_____
_____
_____
_____
_____
_____

DAY 29

- Pray 1-2 hours ☐
- Daily Bible reading ☐
- 30 minutes of Biblical study ☐
- Work on scripture memorization ☐
- One hour or less of media and entertainment ☐

_____
_____
_____
_____
_____
_____
_____
_____
_____
_____
_____
_____
_____
_____

DAY 30

- Pray 1-2 hours ☐
- Daily Bible reading ☐
- 30 minutes of Biblical study ☐
- Work on scripture memorization ☐
- One hour or less of media and entertainment ☐

_____

_____

_____

_____

_____

_____

_____

_____

_____

_____

_____

_____

_____

_____

_____

RECAP

How did your thirty-day prerequisite go? There are a few questions to ponder upon. Once you began to get consistent in prayer, was it easier to go longer in prayer? What verses did you memorize? Did the Word of God become more alive than it had before?

Jeremiah J. Guendoo

Spiritual Boot Camp

In the military, boot camp typically lasts between six to twelve weeks, depending on which branch you join. For our spiritual boot camp, we are going to attempt to go an entire twelve weeks (ninety days). This is a time to put your spiritual walk as the priority in your life. Do not go to sleep without completing every task. Of course, if there is a day where you cannot accomplish everything, have some grace. But then, jump right back into your consistency the next day.

I already know there are some reading this who feel tempted to skip the prerequisite phase and get right into the spiritual boot camp phase. I would highly discourage this. I know some who are reading may have never had a consistent walk with God and are hungry for that consistency. However, jumping right into boot camp without having consistency first will lead to frustration and, ninety-nine percent of the time, result in failure and quitting boot camp. If a person wants to run a marathon, they train for it; they do not decide one day to just start running a marathon out of nowhere.

Listed below are your orders for the ninety days of spiritual boot camp.

Pray two-four Hours a day

Make prayer a priority. Put it above any other tasks, hobbies, or meetings. It is that important. When prayer is a priority, it is easier to go longer into prayer. As a development and lifestyle of prayer is developed with consistency, this becomes easier. "The more you pray, the more you want to pray, and the longer you want to pray" - Verbal Bean.

Daily Bible reading and study for one hour

Let the Word become your life. Listen to it, think upon it, read it. Then after you have read your daily list, study what you have read for 1 hour.

Memorize one verse a week

Fast two-three days a week

Fast two to three days a week. If your lifestyle does not necessitate a water only fast that many days a week, utilize other fast and methods of consecration.

No social media or entertainment

This may be one of the most difficult aspects of boot camp. As previously mentioned, in military boot camp, a soldier often does not have access to social media and communication to the outside world. Often their access to entertainment is limited. Why would a Spiritual boot camp be any different? Cutting off media and entertainment will free up your time to dive deeper into the things of God. (There are of course exceptions for people who must use the internet for things to do with work, or education purposes.)

Once again there will be a daily checklist as well as an area to journal. Just as it was in the prerequisite, there is no daily checkmark for fasting, you will have to find when to fast on your own schedule.

DAY 1

- Pray 2-4 hours ☐
- Daily Bible reading ☐
- 1 hour of Biblical study ☐
- Work on scripture memorization ☐
- No social media and entertainment ☐

_____
_____
_____
_____
_____
_____
_____
_____
_____
_____

DAY 2

- Pray 2-4 hours ☐
- Daily Bible reading ☐
- 1 hour of Biblical study ☐
- Work on scripture memorization ☐
- No social media and entertainment ☐

_____
_____
_____
_____
_____
_____
_____
_____
_____
_____
_____
_____
_____

DAY 3

- Pray 2-4 hours ☐
- Daily Bible reading ☐
- 1 hour of Biblical study ☐
- Work on scripture memorization ☐
- No social media and entertainment ☐

_____

_____

_____

_____

_____

_____

_____

_____

_____

_____

_____

_____

_____

_____

DAY 4

- Pray 2-4 hours ☐
- Daily Bible reading ☐
- 1 hour of Biblical study ☐
- Work on scripture memorization ☐
- No social media and entertainment ☐

_____

_____

_____

_____

_____

_____

_____

_____

_____

_____

_____

_____

_____

DAY 5

- Pray 2-4 hours ☐
- Daily Bible reading ☐
- 1 hour of Biblical study ☐
- Work on scripture memorization ☐
- No social media and entertainment ☐

_____
_____
_____
_____
_____
_____
_____
_____
_____
_____
_____
_____
_____

DAY 6

- Pray 2-4 hours ☐
- Daily Bible reading ☐
- 1 hour of Biblical study ☐
- Work on scripture memorization ☐
- No social media and entertainment ☐

_____
_____
_____
_____
_____
_____
_____
_____
_____
_____
_____
_____
_____

DAY 7

- Pray 2-4 hours ☐
- Daily Bible reading ☐
- 1 hour of Biblical study ☐
- Work on scripture memorization ☐
- No social media and entertainment ☐

_____
_____
_____
_____
_____
_____
_____
_____
_____
_____
_____
_____
_____
_____
_____

DAY 8

- Pray 2-4 hours ☐
- Daily Bible reading ☐
- 1 hour of Biblical study ☐
- Work on scripture memorization ☐
- No social media and entertainment ☐

_____
_____
_____
_____
_____
_____
_____
_____
_____
_____
_____
_____
_____

DAY 9

- Pray 2-4 hours ☐
- Daily Bible reading ☐
- 1 hour of Biblical study ☐
- Work on scripture memorization ☐
- No social media and entertainment ☐

_____
_____
_____
_____
_____
_____
_____
_____
_____
_____
_____
_____
_____
_____

DAY 10

- Pray 2-4 hours ☐
- Daily Bible reading ☐
- 1 hour of Biblical study ☐
- Work on scripture memorization ☐
- No social media and entertainment ☐

_____
_____
_____
_____
_____
_____
_____
_____
_____
_____
_____
_____
_____

DAY 11

- Pray 2-4 hours ☐
- Daily Bible reading ☐
- 1 hour of Biblical study ☐
- Work on scripture memorization ☐
- No social media and entertainment ☐

DAY 12

- Pray 2-4 hours ☐
- Daily Bible reading ☐
- 1 hour of Biblical study ☐
- Work on scripture memorization ☐
- No social media and entertainment ☐

_____
_____
_____
_____
_____
_____
_____
_____
_____
_____
_____
_____
_____

DAY 13

- Pray 2-4 hours ☐
- Daily Bible reading ☐
- 1 hour of Biblical study ☐
- Work on scripture memorization ☐
- No social media and entertainment ☐

_____
_____
_____
_____
_____
_____
_____
_____
_____
_____
_____
_____
_____

DAY 14

- Pray 2-4 hours ☐
- Daily Bible reading ☐
- 1 hour of Biblical study ☐
- Work on scripture memorization ☐
- No social media and entertainment ☐

_____
_____
_____
_____
_____
_____
_____
_____
_____
_____
_____
_____
_____

DAY 15

- Pray 2-4 hours ☐
- Daily Bible reading ☐
- 1 hour of Biblical study ☐
- Work on scripture memorization ☐
- No social media and entertainment ☐

_____
_____
_____
_____
_____
_____
_____
_____
_____
_____
_____
_____
_____
_____

DAY 16

- Pray 2-4 hours ☐
- Daily Bible reading ☐
- 1 hour of Biblical study ☐
- Work on scripture memorization ☐
- No social media and entertainment ☐

DAY 17

- Pray 2-4 hours ☐
- Daily Bible reading ☐
- 1 hour of Biblical study ☐
- Work on scripture memorization ☐
- No social media and entertainment ☐

_____
_____
_____
_____
_____
_____
_____
_____
_____
_____
_____
_____
_____
_____

DAY 18

- Pray 2-4 hours ☐
- Daily Bible reading ☐
- 1 hour of Biblical study ☐
- Work on scripture memorization ☐
- No social media and entertainment ☐

_____
_____
_____
_____
_____
_____
_____
_____
_____
_____
_____
_____
_____

DAY 19

- Pray 2-4 hours ☐
- Daily Bible reading ☐
- 1 hour of Biblical study ☐
- Work on scripture memorization ☐
- No social media and entertainment ☐

_____
_____
_____
_____
_____
_____
_____
_____
_____
_____
_____
_____

DAY 20

- Pray 2-4 hours ☐
- Daily Bible reading ☐
- 1 hour of Biblical study ☐
- Work on scripture memorization ☐
- No social media and entertainment ☐

_____
_____
_____
_____
_____
_____
_____
_____
_____
_____
_____
_____
_____

DAY 21

- Pray 2-4 hours ☐
- Daily Bible reading ☐
- 1 hour of Biblical study ☐
- Work on scripture memorization ☐
- No social media and entertainment ☐

_____
_____
_____
_____
_____
_____
_____
_____
_____
_____
_____
_____
_____

DAY 22

- Pray 2-4 hours ☐
- Daily Bible reading ☐
- 1 hour of Biblical study ☐
- Work on scripture memorization ☐
- No social media and entertainment ☐

_____
_____
_____
_____
_____
_____
_____
_____
_____
_____
_____
_____
_____
_____

DAY 23

- Pray 2-4 hours ☐
- Daily Bible reading ☐
- 1 hour of Biblical study ☐
- Work on scripture memorization ☐
- No social media and entertainment ☐

_____
_____
_____
_____
_____
_____
_____
_____
_____
_____
_____
_____
_____
_____

DAY 24

- Pray 2-4 hours ☐
- Daily Bible reading ☐
- 1 hour of Biblical study ☐
- Work on scripture memorization ☐
- No social media and entertainment ☐

_____
_____
_____
_____
_____
_____
_____
_____
_____
_____
_____
_____
_____

DAY 25

- Pray 2-4 hours ☐
- Daily Bible reading ☐
- 1 hour of Biblical study ☐
- Work on scripture memorization ☐
- No social media and entertainment ☐

_____
_____
_____
_____
_____
_____
_____
_____
_____
_____
_____
_____
_____

DAY 26

- Pray 2-4 hours ☐
- Daily Bible reading ☐
- 1 hour of Biblical study ☐
- Work on scripture memorization ☐
- No social media and entertainment ☐

DAY 27

- Pray 2-4 hours ☐
- Daily Bible reading ☐
- 1 hour of Biblical study ☐
- Work on scripture memorization ☐
- No social media and entertainment ☐

_____

_____

_____

_____

_____

_____

_____

_____

_____

_____

_____

_____

_____

_____

Jeremiah J. Guendoo

DAY 28

- Pray 2-4 hours ☐
- Daily Bible reading ☐
- 1 hour of Biblical study ☐
- Work on scripture memorization ☐
- No social media and entertainment ☐

_____
_____
_____
_____
_____
_____
_____
_____
_____
_____
_____
_____
_____

DAY 29

- Pray 2-4 hours ☐
- Daily Bible reading ☐
- 1 hour of Biblical study ☐
- Work on scripture memorization ☐
- No social media and entertainment ☐

_____
_____
_____
_____
_____
_____
_____
_____
_____
_____
_____
_____

DAY 30

- Pray 2-4 hours ☐
- Daily Bible reading ☐
- 1 hour of Biblical study ☐
- Work on scripture memorization ☐
- No social media and entertainment ☐

_____
_____
_____
_____
_____
_____
_____
_____
_____
_____
_____
_____
_____

DAY 31

- Pray 2-4 hours ☐
- Daily Bible reading ☐
- 1 hour of Biblical study ☐
- Work on scripture memorization ☐
- No social media and entertainment ☐

_____
_____
_____
_____
_____
_____
_____
_____
_____
_____
_____
_____
_____
_____

Jeremiah J. Guendoo

DAY 32

- Pray 2-4 hours ☐
- Daily Bible reading ☐
- 1 hour of Biblical study ☐
- Work on scripture memorization ☐
- No social media and entertainment ☐

_____
_____
_____
_____
_____
_____
_____
_____
_____
_____
_____
_____
_____

DAY 33

- Pray 2-4 hours ☐
- Daily Bible reading ☐
- 1 hour of Biblical study ☐
- Work on scripture memorization ☐
- No social media and entertainment ☐

_____
_____
_____
_____
_____
_____
_____
_____
_____
_____
_____
_____
_____
_____
_____

DAY 34

- Pray 2-4 hours ☐
- Daily Bible reading ☐
- 1 hour of Biblical study ☐
- Work on scripture memorization ☐
- No social media and entertainment ☐

_____
_____
_____
_____
_____
_____
_____
_____
_____
_____
_____
_____

DAY 35

- Pray 2-4 hours ☐
- Daily Bible reading ☐
- 1 hour of Biblical study ☐
- Work on scripture memorization ☐
- No social media and entertainment ☐

_____
_____
_____
_____
_____
_____
_____
_____
_____
_____
_____
_____
_____

Jeremiah J. Guendoo

DAY 36

- Pray 2-4 hours ☐
- Daily Bible reading ☐
- 1 hour of Biblical study ☐
- Work on scripture memorization ☐
- No social media and entertainment ☐

_____
_____
_____
_____
_____
_____
_____
_____
_____
_____
_____
_____

DAY 37

- Pray 2-4 hours ☐
- Daily Bible reading ☐
- 1 hour of Biblical study ☐
- Work on scripture memorization ☐
- No social media and entertainment ☐

_____
_____
_____
_____
_____
_____
_____
_____
_____
_____
_____
_____
_____
_____

DAY 38

- Pray 2-4 hours ☐
- Daily Bible reading ☐
- 1 hour of Biblical study ☐
- Work on scripture memorization ☐
- No social media and entertainment ☐

_____

_____

_____

_____

_____

_____

_____

_____

_____

_____

_____

_____

_____

DAY 39

- Pray 2-4 hours ☐
- Daily Bible reading ☐
- 1 hour of Biblical study ☐
- Work on scripture memorization ☐
- No social media and entertainment ☐

DAY 40

- Pray 2-4 hours ☐
- Daily Bible reading ☐
- 1 hour of Biblical study ☐
- Work on scripture memorization ☐
- No social media and entertainment ☐

_____
_____
_____
_____
_____
_____
_____
_____
_____
_____
_____
_____
_____

DAY 41

- Pray 2-4 hours ☐
- Daily Bible reading ☐
- 1 hour of Biblical study ☐
- Work on scripture memorization ☐
- No social media and entertainment ☐

_____
_____
_____
_____
_____
_____
_____
_____
_____
_____
_____
_____
_____
_____

DAY 42

- Pray 2-4 hours ☐
- Daily Bible reading ☐
- 1 hour of Biblical study ☐
- Work on scripture memorization ☐
- No social media and entertainment ☐

_____
_____
_____
_____
_____
_____
_____
_____
_____
_____
_____
_____
_____

DAY 43

- Pray 2-4 hours ☐
- Daily Bible reading ☐
- 1 hour of Biblical study ☐
- Work on scripture memorization ☐
- No social media and entertainment ☐

_____
_____
_____
_____
_____
_____
_____
_____
_____
_____
_____
_____
_____
_____

DAY 44

- Pray 2-4 hours ☐
- Daily Bible reading ☐
- 1 hour of Biblical study ☐
- Work on scripture memorization ☐
- No social media and entertainment ☐

_____
_____
_____
_____
_____
_____
_____
_____
_____
_____
_____
_____
_____

DAY 45

- Pray 2-4 hours ☐
- Daily Bible reading ☐
- 1 hour of Biblical study ☐
- Work on scripture memorization ☐
- No social media and entertainment ☐

_____
_____
_____
_____
_____
_____
_____
_____
_____
_____
_____
_____
_____
_____

DAY 46

- Pray 2-4 hours ☐
- Daily Bible reading ☐
- 1 hour of Biblical study ☐
- Work on scripture memorization ☐
- No social media and entertainment ☐

_____
_____
_____
_____
_____
_____
_____
_____
_____
_____
_____
_____
_____
_____

DAY 47

- Pray 2-4 hours ☐
- Daily Bible reading ☐
- 1 hour of Biblical study ☐
- Work on scripture memorization ☐
- No social media and entertainment ☐

_____
_____
_____
_____
_____
_____
_____
_____
_____
_____
_____
_____
_____

DAY 48

- Pray 2-4 hours ☐
- Daily Bible reading ☐
- 1 hour of Biblical study ☐
- Work on scripture memorization ☐
- No social media and entertainment ☐

_____
_____
_____
_____
_____
_____
_____
_____
_____
_____
_____
_____

DAY 49

- Pray 2-4 hours ☐
- Daily Bible reading ☐
- 1 hour of Biblical study ☐
- Work on scripture memorization ☐
- No social media and entertainment ☐

_____
_____
_____
_____
_____
_____
_____
_____
_____
_____
_____
_____

DAY 50

- Pray 2-4 hours ☐
- Daily Bible reading ☐
- 1 hour of Biblical study ☐
- Work on scripture memorization ☐
- No social media and entertainment ☐

_____
_____
_____
_____
_____
_____
_____
_____
_____
_____
_____
_____
_____

DAY 51

- Pray 2-4 hours ☐
- Daily Bible reading ☐
- 1 hour of Biblical study ☐
- Work on scripture memorization ☐
- No social media and entertainment ☐

_____
_____
_____
_____
_____
_____
_____
_____
_____
_____
_____
_____
_____

DAY 52

- Pray 2-4 hours ☐
- Daily Bible reading ☐
- 1 hour of Biblical study ☐
- Work on scripture memorization ☐
- No social media and entertainment ☐

_____
_____
_____
_____
_____
_____
_____
_____
_____
_____
_____
_____
_____
_____

DAY 53

- Pray 2-4 hours ☐
- Daily Bible reading ☐
- 1 hour of Biblical study ☐
- Work on scripture memorization ☐
- No social media and entertainment ☐

_____
_____
_____
_____
_____
_____
_____
_____
_____
_____
_____
_____
_____

DAY 54

- Pray 2-4 hours ☐
- Daily Bible reading ☐
- 1 hour of Biblical study ☐
- Work on scripture memorization ☐
- No social media and entertainment ☐

_____
_____
_____
_____
_____
_____
_____
_____
_____
_____
_____
_____
_____

DAY 55

- Pray 2-4 hours ☐
- Daily Bible reading ☐
- 1 hour of Biblical study ☐
- Work on scripture memorization ☐
- No social media and entertainment ☐

_____
_____
_____
_____
_____
_____
_____
_____
_____
_____
_____
_____
_____
_____

DAY 56

- Pray 2-4 hours ☐
- Daily Bible reading ☐
- 1 hour of Biblical study ☐
- Work on scripture memorization ☐
- No social media and entertainment ☐

_____
_____
_____
_____
_____
_____
_____
_____
_____
_____
_____
_____
_____

DAY 57

- Pray 2-4 hours ☐
- Daily Bible reading ☐
- 1 hour of Biblical study ☐
- Work on scripture memorization ☐
- No social media and entertainment ☐

_____
_____
_____
_____
_____
_____
_____
_____
_____
_____
_____
_____
_____

DAY 58

- Pray 2-4 hours ☐
- Daily Bible reading ☐
- 1 hour of Biblical study ☐
- Work on scripture memorization ☐
- No social media and entertainment ☐

_____
_____
_____
_____
_____
_____
_____
_____
_____
_____
_____
_____
_____
_____

DAY 59

- Pray 2-4 hours ☐
- Daily Bible reading ☐
- 1 hour of Biblical study ☐
- Work on scripture memorization ☐
- No social media and entertainment ☐

_____
_____
_____
_____
_____
_____
_____
_____
_____
_____
_____
_____
_____

Jeremiah J. Guendoo

DAY 60

- Pray 2-4 hours ☐
- Daily Bible reading ☐
- 1 hour of Biblical study ☐
- Work on scripture memorization ☐
- No social media and entertainment ☐

DAY 61

- Pray 2-4 hours ☐
- Daily Bible reading ☐
- 1 hour of Biblical study ☐
- Work on scripture memorization ☐
- No social media and entertainment ☐

_____
_____
_____
_____
_____
_____
_____
_____
_____
_____
_____
_____
_____

DAY 62

- Pray 2-4 hours ☐
- Daily Bible reading ☐
- 1 hour of Biblical study ☐
- Work on scripture memorization ☐
- No social media and entertainment ☐

DAY 63

- Pray 2-4 hours ☐
- Daily Bible reading ☐
- 1 hour of Biblical study ☐
- Work on scripture memorization ☐
- No social media and entertainment ☐

_____
_____
_____
_____
_____
_____
_____
_____
_____
_____
_____
_____
_____

DAY 64

- Pray 2-4 hours ☐
- Daily Bible reading ☐
- 1 hour of Biblical study ☐
- Work on scripture memorization ☐
- No social media and entertainment ☐

_____

_____

_____

_____

_____

_____

_____

_____

_____

_____

_____

_____

DAY 65

- Pray 2-4 hours ☐
- Daily Bible reading ☐
- 1 hour of Biblical study ☐
- Work on scripture memorization ☐
- No social media and entertainment ☐

_____
_____
_____
_____
_____
_____
_____
_____
_____
_____
_____
_____
_____

DAY 66

- Pray 2-4 hours ☐
- Daily Bible reading ☐
- 1 hour of Biblical study ☐
- Work on scripture memorization ☐
- No social media and entertainment ☐

_____
_____
_____
_____
_____
_____
_____
_____
_____
_____
_____
_____
_____

DAY 67

- Pray 2-4 hours ☐
- Daily Bible reading ☐
- 1 hour of Biblical study ☐
- Work on scripture memorization ☐
- No social media and entertainment ☐

_____
_____
_____
_____
_____
_____
_____
_____
_____
_____
_____
_____
_____
_____

DAY 68

- Pray 2-4 hours ☐
- Daily Bible reading ☐
- 1 hour of Biblical study ☐
- Work on scripture memorization ☐
- No social media and entertainment ☐

_____

_____

_____

_____

_____

_____

_____

_____

_____

_____

_____

_____

_____

DAY 69

- Pray 2-4 hours ☐
- Daily Bible reading ☐
- 1 hour of Biblical study ☐
- Work on scripture memorization ☐
- No social media and entertainment ☐

_____
_____
_____
_____
_____
_____
_____
_____
_____
_____
_____
_____
_____

DAY 70

- Pray 2-4 hours ☐
- Daily Bible reading ☐
- 1 hour of Biblical study ☐
- Work on scripture memorization ☐
- No social media and entertainment ☐

_____

_____

_____

_____

_____

_____

_____

_____

_____

_____

_____

_____

_____

DAY 71

- Pray 2-4 hours ☐
- Daily Bible reading ☐
- 1 hour of Biblical study ☐
- Work on scripture memorization ☐
- No social media and entertainment ☐

_____

_____

_____

_____

_____

_____

_____

_____

_____

_____

_____

_____

_____

DAY 72

- Pray 2-4 hours ☐
- Daily Bible reading ☐
- 1 hour of Biblical study ☐
- Work on scripture memorization ☐
- No social media and entertainment ☐

_____

_____

_____

_____

_____

_____

_____

_____

_____

_____

_____

_____

_____

DAY 73

- Pray 2-4 hours ☐
- Daily Bible reading ☐
- 1 hour of Biblical study ☐
- Work on scripture memorization ☐
- No social media and entertainment ☐

_____
_____
_____
_____
_____
_____
_____
_____
_____
_____
_____
_____
_____

Jeremiah J. Guendoo

DAY 74

- Pray 2-4 hours ☐
- Daily Bible reading ☐
- 1 hour of Biblical study ☐
- Work on scripture memorization ☐
- No social media and entertainment ☐

DAY 75

- Pray 2-4 hours ☐
- Daily Bible reading ☐
- 1 hour of Biblical study ☐
- Work on scripture memorization ☐
- No social media and entertainment ☐

_____
_____
_____
_____
_____
_____
_____
_____
_____
_____
_____
_____
_____

DAY 76

- Pray 2-4 hours ☐
- Daily Bible reading ☐
- 1 hour of Biblical study ☐
- Work on scripture memorization ☐
- No social media and entertainment ☐

_____
_____
_____
_____
_____
_____
_____
_____
_____
_____
_____
_____
_____

DAY 77

- Pray 2-4 hours ☐
- Daily Bible reading ☐
- 1 hour of Biblical study ☐
- Work on scripture memorization ☐
- No social media and entertainment ☐

_____
_____
_____
_____
_____
_____
_____
_____
_____
_____
_____
_____
_____
_____

DAY 78

- Pray 2-4 hours ☐
- Daily Bible reading ☐
- 1 hour of Biblical study ☐
- Work on scripture memorization ☐
- No social media and entertainment ☐

_____
_____
_____
_____
_____
_____
_____
_____
_____
_____
_____
_____
_____

DAY 79

- Pray 2-4 hours ☐
- Daily Bible reading ☐
- 1 hour of Biblical study ☐
- Work on scripture memorization ☐
- No social media and entertainment ☐

_____
_____
_____
_____
_____
_____
_____
_____
_____
_____
_____
_____
_____
_____

DAY 80

- Pray 2-4 hours ☐
- Daily Bible reading ☐
- 1 hour of Biblical study ☐
- Work on scripture memorization ☐
- No social media and entertainment ☐

_____

_____

_____

_____

_____

_____

_____

_____

_____

_____

_____

_____

_____

DAY 81

- Pray 2-4 hours ☐
- Daily Bible reading ☐
- 1 hour of Biblical study ☐
- Work on scripture memorization ☐
- No social media and entertainment ☐

_____
_____
_____
_____
_____
_____
_____
_____
_____
_____
_____
_____

DAY 82

- Pray 2-4 hours ☐
- Daily Bible reading ☐
- 1 hour of Biblical study ☐
- Work on scripture memorization ☐
- No social media and entertainment ☐

_____
_____
_____
_____
_____
_____
_____
_____
_____
_____
_____
_____
_____

DAY 83

- Pray 2-4 hours ☐
- Daily Bible reading ☐
- 1 hour of Biblical study ☐
- Work on scripture memorization ☐
- No social media and entertainment ☐

_____
_____
_____
_____
_____
_____
_____
_____
_____
_____
_____
_____

DAY 84

- Pray 2-4 hours ☐
- Daily Bible reading ☐
- 1 hour of Biblical study ☐
- Work on scripture memorization ☐
- No social media and entertainment ☐

_____

_____

_____

_____

_____

_____

_____

_____

_____

_____

_____

_____

_____

DAY 85

- Pray 2-4 hours ☐
- Daily Bible reading ☐
- 1 hour of Biblical study ☐
- Work on scripture memorization ☐
- No social media and entertainment ☐

_____
_____
_____
_____
_____
_____
_____
_____
_____
_____
_____
_____
_____
_____

DAY 86

- Pray 2-4 hours ☐
- Daily Bible reading ☐
- 1 hour of Biblical study ☐
- Work on scripture memorization ☐
- No social media and entertainment ☐

_____
_____
_____
_____
_____
_____
_____
_____
_____
_____
_____
_____
_____
_____

DAY 87

- Pray 2-4 hours ☐
- Daily Bible reading ☐
- 1 hour of Biblical study ☐
- Work on scripture memorization ☐
- No social media and entertainment ☐

_____
_____
_____
_____
_____
_____
_____
_____
_____
_____
_____
_____
_____

DAY 88

- Pray 2-4 hours ☐
- Daily Bible reading ☐
- 1 hour of Biblical study ☐
- Work on scripture memorization ☐
- No social media and entertainment ☐

_____
_____
_____
_____
_____
_____
_____
_____
_____
_____
_____
_____
_____

DAY 89

- Pray 2-4 hours ☐
- Daily Bible reading ☐
- 1 hour of Biblical study ☐
- Work on scripture memorization ☐
- No social media and entertainment ☐

_____
_____
_____
_____
_____
_____
_____
_____
_____
_____
_____
_____
_____

DAY 90

- Pray 2-4 hours ☐
- Daily Bible reading ☐
- 1 hour of Biblical study ☐
- Work on scripture memorization ☐
- No social media and entertainment ☐

_____

_____

_____

_____

_____

_____

_____

_____

_____

_____

_____

_____

Recap

If you have made it to the end of this spiritual boot camp, allow me to congratulate you. I know that this was not an easy task to take upon yourself. Think back to what your spiritual life was like before this boot camp. How does it compare now? Do you walk with more faith, victory, joy, and peace? Do you feel you have a better understanding of hearing the voice of God? What about Biblical revelation you have received? God will bless beyond measure any steps we take to get closer to him.

One Year Bible Plan

For the one-year Bible reading daily assignment I have included two plans in this chapter. The first is a 365-day plan from Genesis to Revelation. The second is a 365-day plan with a simultaneous daily read of the Old Testament and New Testament.

Plan 1

Week 1
Gen 1-3
Gen 4-7
Gen 8-11
Gen 12-15
Gen 16-18
Gen 19-21
Gen 22-24

Week 2
Gen 25-26
Gen 27-29
Gen 30-31
Gen 32-33
Gen 34-36
Gen 37-39
Gen 40-41

Week 3
Gen 42-44
Gen 45-46
Gen 47-49
Gen 50; Ex 1-3
Ex 4-6
Ex 7-8
Ex 9-11

Week 4

Ex 12-13
Ex 14-16
Ex 17-20
Ex 21-22
Ex 23-25
Ex 26-28
Ex 29

Week 5
Ex 30-32
Ex 33-35
Ex 36-38
Ex 39-40
Lev 1-4
Lev 5-6
Lev 7-9

Week 6
Lev 10-12
Lev 13
Lev 14-15
Lev 16-17
Lev 18-20
Lev 21-23
Lev 24-25

Week 7
Lev 26-27
Num 1-2
Num 3
Num 4-6
Num 7
Num 8-10
Num 11-13

Week 8
Num 14-15

Num 16-17
Num 18-20
Num 21-22
Num 23-25
Num 26-28
Num 29-30

Week 9
Num 31-32
Num 33-35
Num 36; Deut 1
Deut 2-3
Deut 4-6
Deut 7-9
Deut 10-11

Week 10
Deut 12-14
Deut 15-17
Deut 18-20
Deut 21-23
Deut 24-26
Deut 27-28
Deut 29-30

Week 11
Deut 31-32
Deut 33-34; Josh 1-2
Josh 3-5
Josh 6-7
Josh 8-10
Josh 11-12
Josh 13-16

Week 12
Josh 17-19
Josh 20-22

Josh 23-24
Jdg 1-3
Jdg 4-5
Jdg 6-7
Jdg 8-9

Week 13
Jdg 10-12
Jdg 13-15
Jdg 16-18
Jdg 19
Jdg 20-21; Rut 1
Rut 2-4
1 Sa 1-3

Week 14
1 Sa 4-7
1 Sa 8-9
1 Sa 10-13
1 Sa 14
1 Sa 15-16
1 Sa 17-19
1 Sa 20-21

Week 15
1 Sa 22-24
1 Sa 25-26
1 Sa 27-30
1 Sa 31; 2 Sa 1-2
2 Sa 3-5
2 Sa 6-8
2 Sa 9-11

Week 16
2 Sa 12-13
2 Sa 14-15
2 Sa 16-18

2 Sa 19
2 Sa 20-22
2 Sa 23-24
1 Kgs 1-2

Week 17
1 Kgs 3-4
1 Kgs 5-7
1 Kgs 8
1 Kgs 9-10
1 Kgs 11-12
1 Kgs 13-14
1 Kgs 15-16

Week 18
1 Kgs 17-18
1 Kgs 19-20
1 Kgs 21-22
2 Kgs 1-3
2 Kgs 4
2 Kgs 5-7
2 Kgs 8-9

Week 19
2 Kgs 10-11
2 Kgs 12-14
2 Kgs 15-16
2 Kgs 17-18
2 Kgs 19-20
2 Kgs 21-23
2 Kgs 24-25

Week 20
1 Chr 1-3
1 Chr 4-6
1 Chr 7-8
1 Chr 9-11

1 Chr 12-15
1 Chr 16-18
1 Chr 19-22

Week 21
1 Chr 23-25
1 Chr 26-28
1 Chr 29; 2 Chr 1-2
2 Chr 3-5
2 Chr 6-8
2 Chr 9-12
2 Chr 13-16

Week 22
2 Chr 17-19
2 Chr 20-22
2 Chr 23-25
2 Chr 26-28
2 Chr 29-30
2 Chr 31-32
2 Chr 33-35

Week 23
2 Chr 36; Ezr 1-2
Ezr 3-5
Ezr 6-7
Ezr 8-10
Neh 1-3
Neh 4-6
Neh 7-9

Week 24
Neh 10-11
Neh 12-13
Est 1-4
Est 5-8
Est 9-10; Job 1-2

Job 3-8
Job 9-13

Week 25
Job 14-18
Job 19-23
Job 24-29
Job 30-33
Job 34-38
Job 39-42; Ps 1
Ps 2-10

Week 26
Ps 11-18
Ps 19-26
Ps 27-34
Ps 35-39
Ps 40-47
Ps 48-55
Ps 56-63

Week 27
Ps 64-69
Ps 70-76
Ps 77-80
Ps 81-88
Ps 89-96
Ps 97-104
Ps 105-107

Week 28
Ps 108-117
Ps 118-119
Ps 120-133
Ps 134-142
Ps 143-150; Pro 1
Pro 2-6

Pro 7-11

Week 29
Pro 12-15
Pro 16-19
Pro 20-24
Pro 25-28
Pro 29-31; Ecc 1
Ecc 2-6
Ecc 7-10

Week 30
Ecc 11-12; Sos 1-4
Sos 5-8; Isa 1
Isa 2-5
Isa 6-9
Isa 10-13
Isa 14-18
Isa 19-23

Week 31
Isa 24-27
Isa 28-30
Isa 31-34
Isa 35-37
Isa 38-41
Isa 42-44
Isa 45-48

Week 32
Isa 49-51
Isa 52-56
Isa 57-60
Isa 61-64
Isa 65-66; Jer 1
Jer 2-4
Jer 5-6

Week 33
Jer 7-9
Jer 10-12
Jer 13-15
Jer 16-18
Jer 19-22
Jer 23-24
Jer 25-27

Week 34
Jer 28-29
Jer 30-31
Jer 32-33
Jer 34-36
Jer 37-39
Jer 40-42
Jer 43-45

Week 35
Jer 46-48
Jer 49-50
Jer 51
Jer 52; Lam 1
Lam 2-4
Lam 5; Eze 1-3
Eze 4-6

Week 36
Eze 7-10
Eze 11-13
Eze 14-16
Eze 17-18
Eze 19-20
Eze 21-22
Eze 23-24

Week 37

Eze 25-27
Eze 28-30
Eze 31-32
Eze 33-35
Eze 36-37
Eze 38-39
Eze 40-42

Week 38
Eze 43-44
Eze 45-46
Eze 47-48; Dan 1
Dan 2-3
Dan 4-5
Dan 6-7
Dan 8-9

Week 39
Dan 10-11
Dan 12; Hos 1-4
Hos 5-10
Hos 11-14; Joe 1
Joe 2-3; Amo 1-2
Amo 3-7
Amo 8-9; Oba; Jon 1

Week 40
Jon 2-4; Mic 1-3
Mic 4-7; Nah 1
Nah 2-3; Hab 1-3
Zep 1-3; Hag 1
Hag 2; Zec 1-4
Zec 5-9
Zec 10-14

Week 41
Mal 1-4

Mat 1-4
Mat 5-7
Mat 8-9
Mat 10-12
Mat 13-14
Mat 15-17

Week 42
Mat 18-20
Mat 21-22
Mat 23-24
Mat 25-26
Mat 27-28
Mk 1-3
Mk 4-5

Week 43
Mk 6-8
Mk 9-10
Mk 11-12
Mk 13-14
Mk 15-16
Luk 1-2
Luk 3-4

Week 44
Luk 5-6
Luk 7-8
Luk 9
Luk 10-11
Luk 12-13
Luk 14-16
Luk 17-19

Week 45
Luk 20-21
Luk 22-23

Luk 24; John 1
John 2-4
John 5-6
John 7
John 8-9

Week 46
John 10-11
John 12-14
John 15-17
John 18-19
John 20-21; Acts 1
Acts 2-4
Acts 5-7

Week 47
Acts 8-9
Acts 10-11
Acts 12-13
Acts 14-16
Acts 17-19
Acts 20-21
Acts 22-23

Week 48
Acts 24-26
Acts 27-28; Rom 1
Rom 2-4
Rom 5-8
Rom 9-11
Rom 12-15
Rom 16; 1 Co 1-3

Week 49
1 Co 4-7
1 Co 8-11
1 Co 12-14

1 Co 15-16; 2 Co 1
2 Co 2-6
2 Co 7-10
2 Co 11-13; Gal 1-2

Week 50
Gal 3-5
Gal 6; Eph 1-4
Eph 5-6; Phil 1
Phil 2-4; Col 1
Col 2-4; 1 Th 1-2
1 Th 3-5; 2 Th 1-3
1 Ti 1-6

Week 51
2 Ti 1-4; Tit 1
Tit 2-3; Phlm; Heb 1-3
Heb 4-8
Heb 9-10
Heb 11-13; Jam 1
Jam 2-5
1 Pe 1-5

Week 52
2 Pe 1-3; 1 Jn 1
1 Jn 2-5
2 Jn; 3 Jn; Jude; Rev 1-2
Rev 3-6
Rev 7-10
Rev 11-15
Rev 16-18

Week 53
Rev 19-22

Plan 2

Week 1
Gen 1-2; Mat 1
Gen 3-5; Mat 2
Gen 6-8; Mat 3
Gen 9-11; Mat 4
Gen 12-14
Gen 15-17; Mat 5
Gen 18-19

Week 2
Gen 20-22; Mat 6
Gen 23-24; Mat 7
Gen 25
Gen 26-27; Mat 8
Gen 28-29; Mat 9
Gen 30-31
Gen 32-33; Mat 10

Week 3
Gen 34-35; Mat 11
Gen 36-37
Gen 38-39; Mat 12
Gen 40-41
Gen 42-43
Gen 44-45; Mat 13
Gen 46-47

Week 4

Gen 48-49; Mat 14
Gen 50; Ex 1-2; Mat 15
Ex 3-4
Ex 5-7; Mat 16
Ex 8; Mat 17
Ex 9-11
Ex 12; Mat 18

Week 5
Ex 13-14; Mat 19
Ex 15-16
Ex 17-19; Mat 20
Ex 20-21
Ex 22-23; Mat 21
Ex 24-26
Ex 27-28; Mat 22

Week 6
Ex 29; Mat 23
Ex 30-31
Ex 32-33; Mat 24
Ex 34-35
Ex 36-37; Mat 25
Ex 38-39
Ex 40; Lev 1

Week 7
Lev 2-4; Mat 26
Lev 5-6
Lev 7-8
Lev 9-10; Mat 27
Lev 11-12
Lev 13; Mat 28
Lev 14; Mk 1

Week 8
Lev 15-16

Lev 17-18; Mk 2
Lev 19-20; Mk 3
Lev 21-22
Lev 23-24; Mk 4
Lev 25; Mk 5
Lev 26-27

Week 9
Num 1
Num 2-3; Mk 6
Num 4
Num 5-6; Mk 7
Num 7; Mk 8
Num 8-9
Num 10-11; Mk 9

Week 10
Num 12-13
Num 14-15
Num 16-17; Mk 10
Num 18-19
Num 20-21; Mk 11
Num 22; Mk 12
Num 23-25

Week 11
Num 26-27; Mk 13
Num 28-29
Num 30-31
Num 32; Mk 14
Num 33-34
Num 35-36; Mk 15
Deut 1-2

Week 12
Deut 3-4; Mk 16
Deut 5

Deut 6-7; Luk 1
Deut 8-10
Deut 11; Luk 2
Deut 12-14
Deut 15-16; Luk 3

Week 13
Deut 17-18
Deut 19-21; Luk 4
Deut 22-23
Deut 24-25; Luk 5
Deut 26-27
Deut 28; Luk 6
Deut 29-30

Week 14
Deut 31-32
Deut 33-34; Luk 7
Josh 1-3
Josh 4-6; Luk 8
Josh 7
Josh 8-9
Josh 10; Luk 9

Week 15
Josh 11-13
Josh 14-16
Josh 17-18; Luk 10
Josh 19-21
Josh 22; Luk 11
Josh 23-24
Jdg 1-2

Week 16
Jdg 3-4; Luk 12
Jdg 5-6
Jdg 7-8; Luk 13

Jdg 9
Jdg 10-11; Luk 14
Jdg 12-13; Luk 15
Jdg 14-15

Week 17
Jdg 16-18; Luk 16
Jdg 19; Luk 17
Jdg 20
Jdg 21; Rut 1-2; Luk 18
Rut 3-4
1 Sa 1-2; Luk 19
1 Sa 3-5

Week 18
1 Sa 6-8; Luk 20
1 Sa 9-10; Luk 21
1 Sa 11-12
1 Sa 13-14
1 Sa 15; Luk 22
1 Sa 16-17
1 Sa 18-19; Luk 23

Week 19
1 Sa 20
1 Sa 21-23; Luk 24
1 Sa 24-25
1 Sa 26; John 1
1 Sa 27-29
1 Sa 30-31; 2 Sa 1; John 2
2 Sa 2-3; John 3

Week 20
2 Sa 4-5
2 Sa 6-7; John 4
2 Sa 8-10
2 Sa 11-12; John 5

2 Sa 13-14
2 Sa 15
2 Sa 16-17; John 6

Week 21
2 Sa 18-19
2 Sa 20; John 7
2 Sa 21-22
2 Sa 23-24
1 Kgs 1; John 8
1 Kgs 2
1 Kgs 3-5; John 9

Week 22
1 Kgs 6; John 10
1 Kgs 7
1 Kgs 8; John 11
1 Kgs 9-10
1 Kgs 11-12
1 Kgs 13; John 12
1 Kgs 14-15

Week 23
1 Kgs 16-17; John 13
1 Kgs 18; John 14
1 Kgs 19-20
1 Kgs 21; John 15
1 Kgs 22; 2 Kgs 1; John 16
2 Kgs 2-3
2 Kgs 4; John 17

Week 24
2 Kgs 5-6; John 18
2 Kgs 7-8
2 Kgs 9; John 19
2 Kgs 10-11
2 Kgs 12-13; John 20

2 Kgs 14-15; John 21
2 Kgs 16-17

Week 25
2 Kgs 18; Acts 1
2 Kgs 19-20
2 Kgs 21-22; Acts 2
2 Kgs 23-24; Acts 3
2 Kgs 25; 1 Chr 1
1 Chr 2-3; Acts 4
1 Chr 4-5

Week 26
1 Chr 6-7; Acts 5
1 Chr 8-9; Acts 6
1 Chr 10-11
1 Chr 12-14; Acts 7
1 Chr 15-16
1 Chr 17-20; Acts 8
1 Chr 21-22

Week 27
1 Chr 23-25; Acts 9
1 Chr 26-27
1 Chr 28-29; Acts 10
2 Chr 1-3
2 Chr 4-5; Acts 11
2 Chr 6-7; Acts 12
2 Chr 8-9

Week 28
2 Chr 10-13; Acts 13
2 Chr 14-16
2 Chr 17-18; Acts 14
2 Chr 19-21; Acts 15
2 Chr 22-23
2 Chr 24-25; Acts 16

2 Chr 26-28

Week 29
2 Chr 29; Acts 17
2 Chr 30-31
2 Chr 32-33; Acts 18
2 Chr 34; Acts 19
2 Chr 35-36; Ezr 1
Ezr 2-3; Acts 20
Ezr 4-6

Week 30
Ezr 7; Acts 21
Ezr 8-10
Neh 1-2; Acts 22
Neh 3-4
Neh 5-7; Acts 23
Neh 8; Acts 24
Neh 9-10

Week 31
Neh 11-12; Acts 25
Neh 13; Est 1; Acts 26
Est 2-4
Est 5-7; Acts 27
Est 8-10
Job 1-4; Acts 28
Job 5-8; Rom 1

Week 32
Job 9-12
Job 13-16; Rom 2
Job 17-20; Rom 3
Job 21-24; Rom 4
Job 25-29; Rom 5
Job 30-32; Rom 6
Job 33-35; Rom 7

Week 33
Job 36-38
Job 39-42; Ps 1; Rom 8
Ps 2-8
Ps 9-17; Rom 9
Ps 18-21; Rom 10
Ps 22-27; Rom 11
Ps 28-33; Rom 12

Week 34
Ps 34-37; Rom 13
Ps 38-41; Rom 14
Ps 42-48; Rom 15
Ps 49-54
Ps 55-60; Rom 16
Ps 61-67; 1 Co 1
Ps 68-71; 1 Co 2

Week 35
Ps 72-76; 1 Co 3
Ps 77-78; 1 Co 4
Ps 79-85; 1 Co 5-6
Ps 86-89
Ps 90-96; 1 Co 7
Ps 97-103; 1 Co 8
Ps 104-106; 1 Co 9

Week 36
Ps 107-109
Ps 110-118; 1 Co 10
Ps 119; 1 Co 11
Ps 120-127; 1 Co 12
Ps 128-137; 1 Co 13
Ps 138-144; 1 Co 14
Ps 145-150; Pro 1

Week 37

Pro 2-5
Pro 6-8; 1 Co 15
Pro 9-12; 1 Co 16
Pro 13-15; 2 Co 1
Pro 16-19; 2 Co 2
Pro 20-22; 2 Co 3
Pro 23-25; 2 Co 4

Week 38
Pro 26-29; 2 Co 5
Pro 30-31; Ecc 1; 2 Co 6
Ecc 2-4; 2 Co 7
Ecc 5-7; 2 Co 8
Ecc 8-11; 2 Co 9-10
Ecc 12; Sos 1-4
Sos 5-8; Isa 1; 2 Co 11

Week 39
Isa 2-4; 2 Co 12
Isa 5-7; 2 Co 13
Isa 8-9; Gal 1
Isa 10-13; Gal 2
Isa 14-16; Gal 3
Isa 17-20; Gal 4
Isa 21-23

Week 40
Isa 24-27; Gal 5-6
Isa 28-29; Eph 1
Isa 30-32; Eph 2
Isa 33-35; Eph 3
Isa 36-37; Eph 4
Isa 38-40
Isa 41-43; Eph 5

Week 41
Isa 44-45; Eph 6

Isa 46-48; Phil 1
Isa 49-50; Phil 2
Isa 51-54; Phil 3
Isa 55-57; Phil 4
Isa 58-60
Isa 61-64; Col 1

Week 42
Isa 65-66; Col 2
Jer 1-2; Col 3
Jer 3-4; Col 4; 1 Th 1
Jer 5-6; 1 Th 2
Jer 7-8; 1 Th 3
Jer 9-10; 1 Th 4-5
Jer 11-13; 2 Th 1

Week 43
Jer 14-15; 2 Th 2
Jer 16-17; 2 Th 3; 1 Ti 1
Jer 18-20; 1 Ti 2
Jer 21-22; 1 Ti 3-4
Jer 23-25; 1 Ti 5
Jer 26; 1 Ti 6
Jer 27-29; 2 Ti 1

Week 44
Jer 30; 2 Ti 2
Jer 31-32; 2 Ti 3
Jer 33; 2 Ti 4; Tit 1
Jer 34-35; Tit 2
Jer 36-37; Tit 3; Phlm
Jer 38-40; Heb 1
Jer 41-42; Heb 2

Week 45
Jer 43-44; Heb 3
Jer 45-47; Heb 4-5

Jer 48-49; Heb 6
Jer 50; Heb 7
Jer 51; Heb 8
Jer 52; Heb 9
Lam 1-2

Week 46
Lam 3-5; Heb 10
Eze 1-3
Eze 4-6; Heb 11
Eze 7-8; Heb 12
Eze 9-11
Eze 12-13; Heb 13
Eze 14-15; Jam 1

Week 47
Eze 16-17; Jam 2
Eze 18-19; Jam 3
Eze 20; Jam 4-5
Eze 21-22
Eze 23; 1 Pe 1
Eze 24-26; 1 Pe 2
Eze 27-28; 1 Pe 3

Week 48
Eze 29-30; 1 Pe 4
Eze 31-32; 1 Pe 5; 2 Pe 1
Eze 33
Eze 34-36; 2 Pe 2
Eze 37; 2 Pe 3; 1 Jn 1
Eze 38-39; 1 Jn 2
Eze 40

Week 49
Eze 41-43; 1 Jn 3
Eze 44; 1 Jn 4
Eze 45-46; 1 Jn 5

Eze 47-48; 2 Jn; 3 Jn
Dan 1-2; Jude
Dan 3; Rev 1
Dan 4-5

Week 50
Dan 6; Rev 2
Dan 7-8; Rev 3
Dan 9-10; Rev 4
Dan 11-12; Rev 5
Hos 1-4; Rev 6
Hos 5-8; Rev 7
Hos 9-13; Rev 8

Week 51
Hos 14; Joe 1-2; Rev 9
Joe 3; Amo 1-2; Rev 10
Amo 3-6; Rev 11
Amo 7-9; Rev 12
Oba; Jon 1-3; Rev 13
Jon 4; Mic 1-4; Rev 14
Mic 5-7; Rev 15

Week 52
Nah 1-3; Hab 1; Rev 16
Hab 2-3; Zep 1; Rev 17
Zep 2-3; Hag 1-2; Rev 18
Zec 1-3; Rev 19
Zec 4-8; Rev 20
Zec 9-11
Zec 12-14; Rev 21

Week 53
Mal 1-4; Rev 22

About The Author

Jeremiah Guendoo, along with his wife, Joy, and daughter, Jael, travel full-time as international Evangelist's. They have a love and passion to see revival ignited in the hearts of churches, as souls receive the Holy Ghost, are miracles, deliverance, and are water baptized in Jesus name. He is licensed with the United Pentecostal Church International.

For other books that Jeremiah Guendoo has written, or if you want to inquire more about the ministry, please visit

jeremiahjguendoo.com

or email

evgjguendoo@gmail.com

About The Author

Made in the USA
Middletown, DE
16 March 2024

51020675R00106